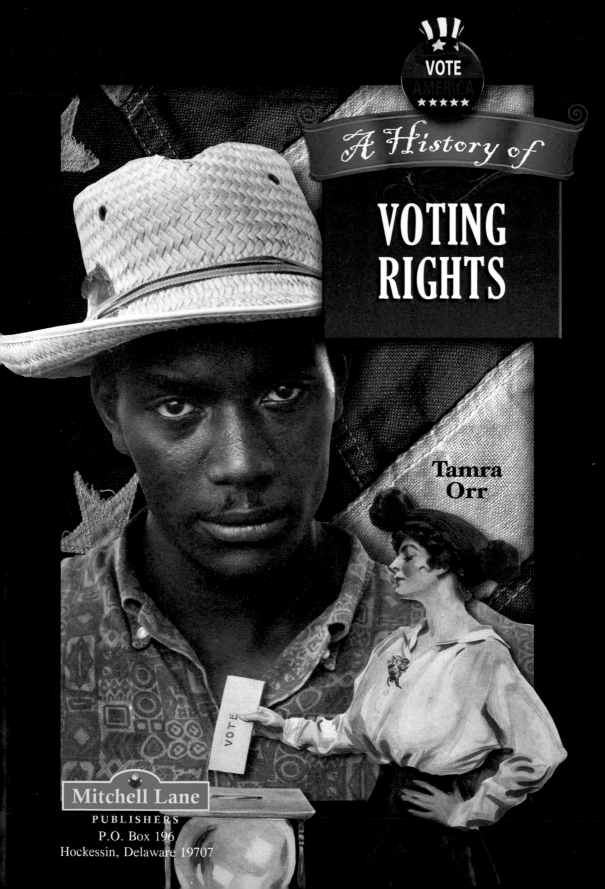

VOTE
AMERICA
★★★★★

A History of

VOTING RIGHTS

Tamra
Orr

Mitchell Lane
PUBLISHERS
P.O. Box 196
Hockessin, Delaware 19707

A History of the Democratic Party
A History of the Republican Party
A History of Voting Rights
A Kid's Guide to the Voting Process

Printing   1   2   3   4   5   6   7   8   9

Library of Congress Cataloging-in-Publication Data

Orr, Tamra.
 A history of voting rights / by Tamra Orr.
   p. cm. — (Vote America)
 Includes bibliographical references and index.
 ISBN 978-1-61228-262-6 (library bound)
 1. Suffrage—United States—History—Juvenile literature. 2. Voting—United States—History—Juvenile literature. 3. African Americans—Suffrage—History—Juvenile literature. 4. Women—Suffrage—United States—History—Juvenile literature. I. Title.
 JK1846.O77 2012
 362.6'20973—dc23
                                          2012007540
 eBook ISBN: 9781612283395
                                          PLB

CONTENTS

Chapter 1

Early Voting Rights

The deck of the ship was windy and cold, but no one seemed to notice. The rough seas from the day before had finally calmed, and everyone was grateful. For this moment, at least, the ship had stopped heaving over pounding waves. The smooth sailing brought new hope to the voyagers, who had spent days in their bunks, too sick to do anything but wait for their journey to end.

Pockets of people stood together, chatting about the journey. Eager eyes watched for signs of land on the horizon. Everywhere there was excitement about the new life that was waiting across the dark water. Almost every passenger had the same goal: freedom. These travelers wanted the freedom to live as they pleased and to make their own decisions. For too many years, they had been under the control of a king who did not care about their beliefs or concerns. They had no voice in decisions that were made. They longed for a home where they could have more freedom.

After arriving on a new shore, people scattered to different areas, slowly forming thirteen colonies. Although each one of these new regions was somewhat

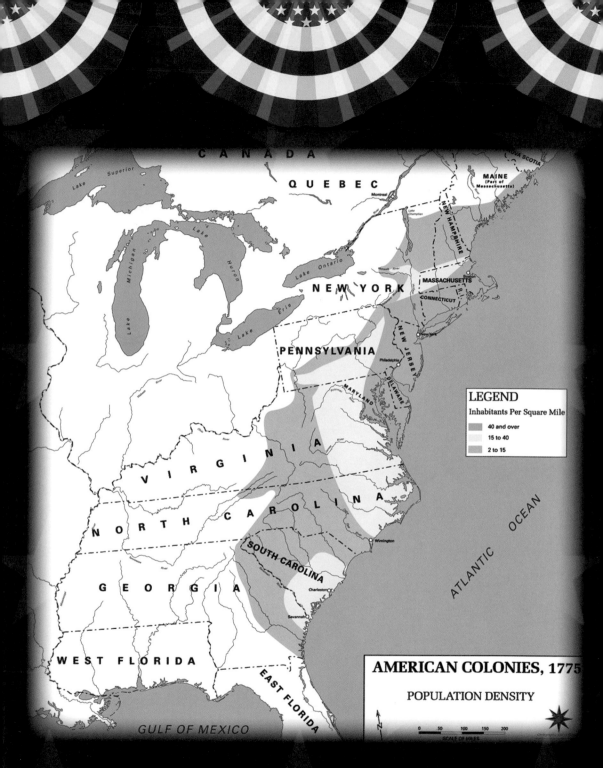

The population of the American colonies in 1775 was focused along the coast. Over the years, it would slowly expand into the western regions.

People filled the streets, protesting the Stamp Act, which forced them to pay taxes to England and yet had no say in what decisions the British parliament made.

independent, they all still modeled themselves after British customs and ideas, and were largely under British control. The population grew, schools were built, newspapers were established, and leaders were appointed.

As time passed, the people in these colonies found themselves chafing under British rule and laws. After the Stamp Act was passed in 1765, these colonists were forced to pay taxes directly to England on all paper items, from newspapers to contracts and other documents, as well as on dice and even playing cards. The colonists were angry, and they became even more so when they were told that they had to house British troops and supply them with food. Despite these rules, the colonists were not allowed to object or to have any say in the crown's rulings.

When they refused to cooperate, England declared that it had total power to pass any laws controlling the colonies. Known as "taxation without representation," the move sparked the colonists to talk seriously about rebellion. The disagreement escalated. In May 1773, another tax was added to the colonists—this time on tea. A group of angry colonists refused to pay it. Instead, disguised as Native Americans, they boarded the British ships and dumped 342 containers of tea into Boston Harbor.

The fight was on. In summer 1775 the first battle broke out in the Revolutionary War (1775-1781). The colonists drafted a document that created a new nation—the United States of America. When England was defeated, the new country drew up the U.S. Constitution and the Bill of Rights.

"The Constitution is not an instrument for the government to restrain the people, it is an instrument for the people to restrain the government—lest it come to dominate our lives and interests."—Patrick Henry

The colonists tolerated a great deal from England, but when it attempted to tax their tea, they had had enough. The Boston Tea Party was one of the key events that sparked the Revolutionary War.

Having a Voice

Have you thought about what it will be like to one day cast your first vote in a state or national election? Voting has been such a natural part of this nation's culture that chances are you may not have given it much thought. However, it is extremely important to this country's history and the way its government operates.

The right to vote is actually the right to have a voice in all kinds of decisions, big and small, local and national. By voting for one person or against another one, you are saying that you agree or disagree with how that person will vote on important issues. You are saying yes or no to spending more or less money on a cause, project, or program. You are saying yes or no to what should be done about such controversial issues as abortion, gay rights, and capital punishment.

When people talk about their "rights," the Declaration of Independence or the U.S. Constitution often comes to mind. After all, the Declaration practically begins with promises of "the right to life, liberty and the pursuit of happiness," and the Constitution includes the Bill of Rights. This important document spells out essential American freedoms, including freedom of religion and freedom of speech. It also explains how leaders shall be voted into office. But what do these documents say about the right to vote?

Perhaps surprisingly, the Constitution does not state that people *have* the right to vote, only that they *cannot be denied* the right to vote. When the Founding Fathers first wrote that rule, the group of people who were guaranteed the right to vote in these documents was actually rather limited. Many different groups were left out. The document left the decision about who could and could not cast a vote to the individual states. Why?

Educated men such as John Hancock, Benjamin Franklin, George Washington, and Thomas Jefferson helped to draft and write the Constitution. They knew that the people were desperately eager for a government that would not have too much control over their lives. The war with Great Britain over the question of control was still fresh. These rebels wanted to live without interference from a king or other type of big government. They knew that the more responsibility this new nation could leave up to the people within its individual states, the happier everyone would be.

The first election in the United States was held in January 1789, when George Washington was elected as the first U.S. president. The only people who were allowed to vote at this time were white men over the age of 18 who owned property. This included only about 6 percent of the country's population.[1] What about the country's other citizens?

The following year, in 1790, another law regarding voting was passed. Known as the Naturalization Law, this law stated that any

Writing the Declaration of Independence was an extremely difficult and passion-filled process. Some of history's wisest, most experienced men labored over every single word, knowing how important each phrase would be to the people of the nation.

"free white person" who lived in the United States could be considered a citizen and allowed to vote. The law added that the person must be "of good character."[2] He also had to be male.

It took years of hard work and several amendments to the U.S. Constitution to guarantee this right for everyone. For many years, voting was denied to African Americans, Native Americans, and women of all races. The story of the fight for their rights as citizens is a key thread throughout U.S. history.

George Washington is memorialized in Washington Square in Philadelphia, Pennsylvania. As the first elected president of the United States, Washington has a number of memorials dedicated to him throughout the country.

Blacks and Citizenship Rights

For ten frustrating years, Dred Scott had been fighting. He had lost count of how many times he had walked into a courtroom or filed an appeal trying to gain his freedom. He had spent most of his life as a slave, largely in states where slavery was illegal. In 1843, he and his wife approached their owner with $300 to buy their freedom. They were denied. Not sure what to do next, Scott turned to the justice system. He would sue the owners for freedom. In 1850, the St. Louis court agreed with Scott: the couple was free.

Victory was short-lived. Just two years later, the Missouri Supreme Court reversed that decision—the couple was not free. Finally, Scott took the case to the U.S. Supreme Court. He was devastated when he lost there too. The Supreme Court ruled that since Scott was black, he was not a citizen and had no legal ability to sue.[1] It was a huge blow to Scott—and to all black Americans.

North versus South: The Civil War

Not all of the passengers who crossed the ocean to North America were excited about the journey.

Dred Scott dedicated most of his life to obtaining freedom. Tragically, only nine months after he finally received it, he died.

Freedom was actually the last thing they were being given, so they were not full of hope and excitement for a new life. Instead, they were thinking about the freedom that had been taken away. They came packed tightly in the ships' holds, and they were terrified and confused. These Africans were slaves, and the rights they sought, from simply being free to having the right to vote, were many years away.

Slavery was a part of American life for many years throughout the United States. When Abraham Lincoln became president, he led the country in a battle fought within its own borders. The Civil War (1861–1865) was fought for many reasons, and bringing an end to slavery was one of them. In Lincoln's Emancipation Proclamation, he declared for the year 1863, "That on the first day of January, . . . all persons held as slaves within any state . . . shall be then, thenceforward, and forever free."[2]

When the war finally ended in 1865, more than 4 million slaves were given their freedom, but that did not mean they suddenly had the same rights as whites. Until this point, in the census that counted all Americans, each of the slaves had only been considered to be three-fifths of a person! The Fourteenth Amendment, passed in 1868, stated that African Americans were now full citizens. However, just because the law said that the races were equal did not mean people agreed with the idea. Many white people still saw former slaves as inferior. They suspected that black people were not as smart as whites. They believed that these former slaves were simply not responsible enough to hold jobs and go to school—or to vote.

Two years later, the government added another amendment to the Constitution. Although the previous amendment granted citizenship to blacks, it did not stop discrimination against them based on their race. More was needed to get this in motion. The Fifteenth Amendment made it clear that blacks were indeed free to vote, stating that voting "shall not be denied or abridged by the United States or by any State on account of race, color, or

President Lincoln was much loved by many of the nation's black citizens as he brought them their eventual freedom, beginning with the signing of the Emancipation Proclamation on September 22, 1862.

The First Vote, drawn by A. R. Waud for the cover of Harper's Weekly in 1867, shows an African American man casting his ballot. In reality, the first black vote would not be cast for three more years.

previous condition of servitude."[3] Although this brought an end to the debate on paper, it did not solve the problems blacks were still facing on a daily basis. In fact, the situation got far worse before it got better.

Now that they had the right to vote, many blacks turned out to elections in large numbers. They wanted the chance to vote and share their opinions about possible leaders. However, many whites, especially those in the Southern states where the loss of the Civil War was still painful, believed that letting blacks vote was a huge mistake. They did everything they could to stop blacks from casting their votes.

Putting Up Barriers

Right after the Civil War ended, federal troops were scattered throughout the South to help the area rebuild. This period was known as the Reconstruction. While these soldiers were around, blacks were usually given a fair chance to find jobs, own homes, and get involved in politics, thanks to the 1875 Civil Rights Act. However, by 1877, federal troops had left the South. Without the government's protection, African Americans were faced daily with anger and violence, and in 1883, the Supreme Court decided the Act was unconstitutional. The court took those rights back.

Having the right to vote was important, but it did not mean much if the right could not be exercised. Many blacks were threatened when they arrived to vote. They were told that they or their families would be beaten or their homes would be burned to the ground. Their jobs were threatened also. Frightened for their safety, many of them went home without casting a single vote.

Another method of keeping blacks away from the voting booths was setting up a poll tax. This was a fee that all citizens had to pay in order to vote. Some of the states set this fee high enough that many blacks simply could not afford to pay it.

A third method was giving a literacy test, or checking each voter's ability to read, before allowing that person to vote. People

No. 1336   **Poll Tax Receipt, 189 5**

Office of Collector of Garland Co., Ark., 4 9 1895

RECEIVED OF W. F. Crawford

One Dollar in payment of Poll Tax charged against him for year 189

Collector Garland County, Ark.

Brown Printing Co., Little Rock—1894.

D. C.

A poll tax receipt from 1895

were asked to read out loud and explain what the passage meant in order to prove they were educated. Quite often they had to read a section of the Constitution. Because many blacks had lived the majority of their lives as slaves, they did not know how to read. Most had never been to school. They could not possibly pass a literacy test. Some of the registrars at the polls deliberately chose the hardest parts of the Constitution for blacks to read, knowing that it would be impossible for them. Many blacks did not even try.

Not all of the white people in these towns were able to read or afford the poll tax either. What about them? Were they allowed to vote? Often they were, thanks to a loophole called the grandfather's clause. This law stated that if a person's father or grandfather had voted in past elections, that person could vote too, without having to pay the tax or read. Once again, blacks

VOTE

Voting is a chance to stand up and voice your opinion, to have a say in what goes on in your city, your state, and your country as a whole. It is a right that U.S. citizens who are over the age of 18 are guaranteed. Be sure to use it. After all—it's your right!

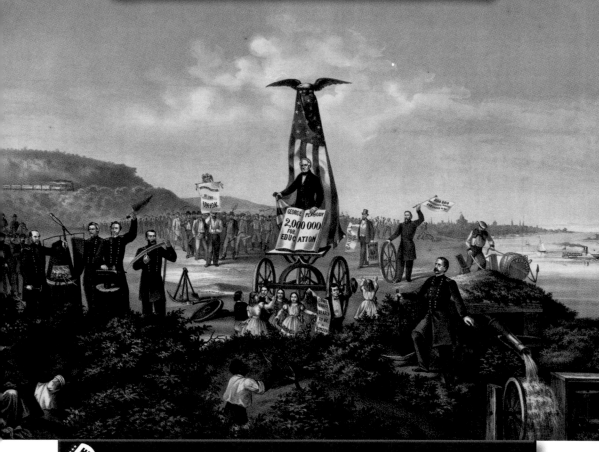

Reconstruction was a slow process, and many people disagreed on what was most important to change and in what order!

were left out because even if they were free, it was unlikely that their fathers or grandfathers had been.

All of these barriers made it very difficult and often frightening for blacks to attempt to vote. Some of them went to court, outraged that this right was being denied. Often they won in court, but it did not make much of a difference. A judge could rule in a black person's favor, but he could not enforce that ruling out on the streets, where it counted most.

Chapter 3

Blacks and the Right to Vote

For the cooks and servers at the F.W. Woolworth store in Greensboro, North Carolina, February 1, 1960, seemed like any other day. They reported to work and started doing their jobs. They had no way of knowing that before this day ended, the world would be talking about their store and what happened there.

On this day, four brave 17-year-olds who went to school at the all-black Agricultural and Technical College of North Carolina walked into F. W. Woolworth Co. and took a seat at the luncheon counter to order some food. Silence settled over the restaurant. Everyone there knew that blacks simply were not allowed in this restaurant. Their order was ignored and the students were told to leave.

The students didn't leave. They sat there all day, and the next morning, they came back with friends. They were ignored.

They came back the next day—and by the end of the week, there were 1,000 protesters on both sides of the issue outside Woolworth's.[1] But the message got through. By July 25, 1960, the F.W. Woolworth lunch counter was desegregated.[2]

The four young men who walked into Woolworth's in 1960 are still considered some of history's biggest heroes.

This passive "sit-in" was a nonviolent way to say, "No! I am a citizen and I want my rights." The four young men in North Carolina had started a new movement, and by April 1960, many cities in more than a dozen states had had sit-ins also.[3]

Sometimes getting the rights you deserve takes a great deal of bravery and even breaking a few rules. That is what these four students proved that day long ago in Woolworth's.

The Civil Rights Movement

Whites became much more used to living with free blacks. Slowly, slavery became a part of the past. Problems with equality continued, however. In Alabama, officials redrew the boundaries of a city so that the city no longer included black neighborhoods. People who lived outside the new boundaries were unable to vote. When African Americans took the issue to court, they won, and the city's borders went back to how they were originally.

In 1962, another amendment was added to the Constitution that helped blacks get closer to their full voting rights. The Twenty-fourth Amendment, passed in 1964, barred any state from using a poll tax in a federal election. Although local state elections could still use them, poll taxes slowly began to fade until they completely disappeared across the country.

Although this amendment was supposed to help blacks in their battle for equality, it also made things more difficult for many of them. Leaders like Malcolm X and Martin Luther King Jr. encouraged

Malcolm X

Ratified amendment, 1962–1964

Ratified amendment post-enactment, 1977, 1989, 2002, 2009*

Rejected amendment

Did not ratify amendment

*Years are 1977—Virginia; 1989—North Carolina; 2002—Alabama; and 2009—Texas

Most states ratified the Twenty-fourth Amendment in the early 1960s, but several states rejected it or didn't ratify it, while others took a decade or almost 50 years to do so.

African Americans to get involved in politics. They urged them to vote in every election. A number of Americans were uncomfortable with this level of involvement from blacks. There were riots and violence. On February 21, 1965, Malcolm X was assassinated.

On March 7, 1965, a date that later became known as "Bloody Sunday," 600 civil rights marchers gathered. They began walking east from the city of Selma, Alabama. As they reached Edmund Pettus Bridge, just a couple of blocks away, local police attacked. Billy clubs were swung. Tear gas was sprayed. More than 60 people were injured. Just two days later, Martin Luther King Jr. led 1,500 people on another march. When they reached the bridge, state police were waiting. Marchers quickly disbanded. Finally, on March 21, a third march was organized. It began with 3,200 marchers. They walked 12 miles a day, and by the time they reached Montgomery, there were more than 25,000 people.[4] This proved to

The people who participated in the civil rights march from Selma to Montgomery in 1965 were trying to change the world in a nonviolent way. Their message was sent loud and clear.

President Johnson, Martin Luther King Jr., and Rosa Parks were all present for the signing of the Voting Rights Act on August 6, 1965. It was a moment in history that changed the way people thought and behaved.

the White House, and to the rest of the nation, that it was time for a new Civil Rights Act.

Shortly after, President Lyndon B. Johnson signed the Civil Rights Act of 1965. It made literacy tests and poll taxes illegal in all elections. In a speech to the nation, Johnson said, "Today is a triumph for freedom as huge as any victory that has ever been won on any battlefield. . . . This act flows from a clear and simple wrong. Its only purpose is to right that wrong. Millions of Americans are denied the right to vote because of their color. This law will ensure them the right to vote."[5]

The number of registered black voters began to soar in all states of the country, even in the South. African Americans were also elected into more and more public offices. Finally, the right to vote was shared fully with black people. At last, their voices were heard.

Chapter 4

Women and the Right to Vote

When former slave Sojourner Truth walked up on the stage of the Akron, Ohio Women's Convention in 1851, the room quieted. All day, people had been listening to women explain why they deserved the right to equality and the right to vote. Now it was this woman's turn. With passion and power, she began to speak, capturing everyone's attention with her words.

"Look at me!" she shouted. "Look at my arm! I have ploughed and planted, and gathered into barns, and no man could head me! And ain't I a woman? I could work as much and eat as much as a man—when I could get it—and bear the lash as well! And ain't I a woman?" People began nodding. Truth continued, "If the first woman God ever made was strong enough to turn the world upside down all alone, these women together ought to be able to turn it back, and get it right side up again! And now they is asking to do it, the men better let them!"[1]

Sojourner Truth was only one of the women's voices that were raised across the country demanding the right to vote. Although the voices started softly, they soon became a loud wave that washed over the nation, making changes as it went.

Sojourner Truth's impassioned words helped people realize that women were equal citizens who deserved equal rights—including the right to decide who should lead the country.

Equality for All?

Before the Civil War began, a number of women were involved in fighting for the freedom of slaves. These abolitionists believed that the races were created equally. They campaigned for slavery to come to an end. It came as little surprise that, as these women worked for racial equality, they began to also want gender equality. In many ways, the two issues were quite similar.

Two women, Lucretia Mott, a Quaker minister, and Elizabeth Cady Stanton, a writer, began focusing on the rights of women. Together, they organized the first women's rights convention. It was held over two days in Seneca Falls, New York, during the summer of 1848. The two women were joined by a passionate teacher and speaker named Susan B. Anthony. Over time, she would become one of the most well known suffragists in the country. She is often thought of as the mother of the entire movement. Another supporter at the convention was African American Frederick Douglass. He not only spoke at meetings for the importance of women's rights, but also wrote about it in newspapers.

More than 300 people attended this convention. Before the meeting was over, 68 women and 32 men wrote the Declaration of Sentiments. It stated, "The history of mankind is a history of repeated injuries and usurpations on the part of

Lucretia Mott

The combination of Susan B. Anthony (left) and Elizabeth Cady Stanton was amazing—as well as persuasive.

man toward woman, having in direct object the establishment of an absolute tyranny over her."[2] Then the document listed the many different ways men held power over women, including not letting women vote, own property, or seek divorces.

Two years later, the first annual National Women's Rights Convention was held in Worcester, Massachusetts. This time more than

"It was we, the people; not we, the white male citizens; nor yet we, the male citizens; but we, the whole people, who formed the Union. . . . Men, their rights and nothing more; women, their rights and nothing less." ~Susan B. Anthony

1,000 people attended from almost a dozen different states. The movement was slowly gaining in numbers, but it had a long way to go.

An Arrest

When the nation entered the Civil War, the suffragist movement had to pause. Women were far too busy caring for the wounded and supporting slaves seeking freedom to battle for their own rights. These women celebrated along with the country's blacks when the war ended and slaves were set free. However, as pleased as they were, women were also furious because their rights had been ignored again. Blacks were on their way to gaining equality, but women had been left behind once more. Too many people still believed that the "fairer sex" was too fragile and not quite smart enough to handle a responsibility like voting.

In 1872, Anthony had had enough. She wanted to vote in the presidential election—so she did. For two weeks, she thought perhaps she had gotten away with breaking the law, but then she was arrested. So were the women who had gone with her and the voting inspectors who had allowed them in. When she appeared in court, Anthony was not allowed to speak in her defense, and the judge declared her guilty without even allowing the jury to deliberate.

When it came time to sentence her, she was given the chance to speak. She accused the judge of ignoring her rights. When he fined her $100, she replied, "I shall never pay a dollar of your unjust penalty. . . . And I shall earnestly and persistently continue to urge all women . . . that resistance to tyranny is obedience to

God."[3] Her courage in the face of the court won her a great deal of respect around the world.

Slow Changes and Long Pauses

Years went by and nothing changed, despite the hard work of Anthony, Stanton, Mott, Douglass, and many others. Several national groups formed, and in 1890 they merged to form the National American Woman Suffrage Association. At the same time, more and more families were moving into the unexplored western areas of the country. There, pioneer women were proving to everyone that they had the strength and endurance to handle a rough life. Weak and inferior they were not!

As the nineteenth century ended and the twentieth began, women still did not have the right to vote. In 1913, thousands of people banded together to fight for women's rights. They had parades through cities like New York City and Washington, D.C. They picketed

WE DEMAND
AN AMENDMENT TO
THE
UNITED STATES
CONSTITUTION
ENFRANCHISING
WOMEN

WELCOME
SUFFRAGE ENVOYS

The fight for voting rights for women was a slow one. Year after year passed and little progress was made, despite the dedication and efforts of countless women. In the end, it was their perseverance that helped them achieve equal rights.

the White House too. Many of them were arrested and thrown in jail, and a number of them went on hunger strikes to protest.

Just as the movement seemed to be making progress, another national crisis interfered. This time it was World War I (1914–1918). Women set aside their passion for equal rights and concentrated instead on nursing injured soldiers. They also took on the jobs that men had traditionally held, from firefighting and farming to teaching and working in factories. They filled in wherever they were needed, and their ability to do so helped to prove to many people that women were as strong and capable as men.

At long last, in 1920, the Nineteenth Amendment was added to the Constitution, and women were given the right to vote. In the first election following its ratification, more than 26 million women voted.[4]

One Last Minority

It took decades, but finally African Americans and women had achieved their full rights as American citizens. Ironically, the group that still wasn't allowed to vote was the people who had been in the country longer than anyone else—the Native Americans. Some of them had earned citizenship through marriage, and others through treaties, but many still were barred from their rights. It was not until 1924 that the federal government finally passed the Indian Citizenship Act. Dr. Joseph K. Dixon wrote at the time: "The Indian, though a man without a country, the Indian who has suffered a thousand wrongs considered the white man's burden and from mountains, plains, and divides, the Indian threw himself into the struggle. . . . Now, shall we not redeem ourselves by redeeming all the tribes?"[5] That redemption came—but it took a very long time.

U.S. President Calvin Coolidge stands on the White House lawn with four Osage Indians after he signed the bill granting Native Americans full citizenship.

Chapter 5

Current Voting Issues

If you ask most Americans whether voting rights are equal for everyone in this country, you are most likely going to see a puzzled frown and a nod of the head. With all races and genders holding the right to vote, what other problems could there be? Surprisingly enough, there are several, and each of them goes back to the same issue of just who does and does not have citizenship.

Questions to Ponder
Over the years, all minority citizens have been given the right to vote. By 2012, however, there were two other minorities that were fighting for that right, and so far, they have not won. They are former and current felons and recent immigrants.

People who have been convicted of a felony face many consequences. They often cannot buy firearms or serve on a jury. They cannot be given welfare or federal money, and they may have trouble getting a job or renting a place to live. Felons also lose the right to vote. Is that fair?

Many people on both sides of the issue have strong feelings about it. A felon's loss of the right to vote is

In 2011, an inmate at Matrosskaya Tishina prison was allowed to cast a vote in the Moscow election. In the United States, however, that right is taken away from prisoners—and from many of those who have been released.

In 1993, President Bill Clinton signed the National Voter Registration Act, also called the Motor Voter Act. In an effort to get more eligible voters involved in elections, this act allows qualified citizens to register to vote when they apply for or renew their driver's license, or when they apply for social services. This makes it much easier for low-income and minority citizens to become registered voters.

known as criminal disenfranchisement. Whether or not felons are allowed to vote once they have served their sentences and been released depends on the state in which they live. Only a couple of states have no disenfranchisement (Maine and Vermont). A little over a dozen states restore voting rights to convicts as soon as they have been released from prison. Another two dozen allow former inmates to vote once they have completed their prison sentence plus any parole or probation they have been given. Permanent disenfranchisement exists in ten states. These laws affect millions of people.

A number of people are fighting this denial of the right to vote. In 2009, Senator Russell Feingold and Representative John Conyers proposed the Democracy Restoration Act. It is designed to restore voting rights in federal elections to former convicts throughout the country. The decision of whether or not it would pass into law was slated to be made sometime in mid-2012.

The second group of people who want the right to vote but have not necessarily been granted it are legal immigrants who have not yet become citizens. There are about 10 million people throughout the United States who fall into this category. Their right to vote is a hotly debated topic in many parts of the country. On one side of the issue, people believe that these residents should be able to vote. "They may be aliens from a national or international perspective," Professor Jamin Raskin, American University law professor, told *The New York Times*, "but locally they are taxpayers, neighbors and parents of kids in school." Others believe that no one should have the right to vote without first becoming a U.S. citizen. "No one should be given the franchise without taking the Pledge of Allegiance," Daniel Stein, executive director of the Federation for American Immigration Reform, said in the same article. "If you divorce citizenship and voting, citizenship stops having any meaning at all."[1]

Another voting rights question is whether Americans currently living in other countries should have the right to vote in U.S. elections. Millions of Americans live in U.S. dependencies—places such as Puerto Rico, the Virgin Islands, and Guam. They also cannot vote in presidential elections. Should they be able to? It is a question many different organizations discuss and debate.

Two Other Issues to Consider

Along with these two groups who are fighting to get voting rights, two additional issues have come up in recent years that have a direct effect on voting rights. The first one is voter identification (ID), and the second is mandatory voting.

In a growing number of states, it is necessary to have an official government-issued ID with your picture on it in order to be allowed to vote. The reason behind this law is to prevent voter fraud—voting under a false name. While many people have no trouble pulling out a state-issued ID, a driver's license, or a passport to prove who they are, others may struggle to provide such identification. In fact, one study reported that as many as one in ten people would not have the proper kind of ID.[2]

Many experts believe that having to provide this ID will make it harder for some people to vote. Senator Richard J. Durbin, Democrat of Illinois, stated in *The New York Times* that it "will make it harder for millions of disabled, young, minority, rural, elderly, homeless and low-income Americans to vote."[3]

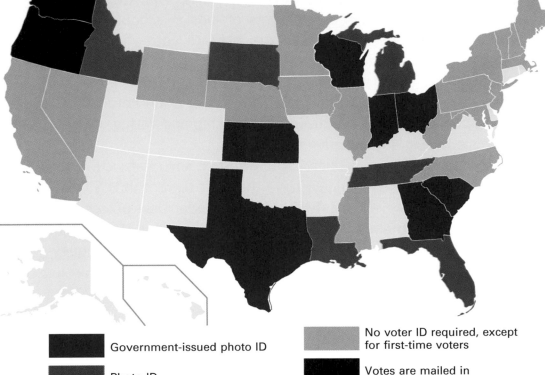

Government-issued photo ID

No voter ID required, except for first-time voters

Photo ID

Votes are mailed in

ID, non-photo accepted. In many cases, a signed affidavit, or recognition by a person with voter ID, will suffice.

As of January 2012, the voter ID laws in the United States were still divided. A number of states still have not made it necessary for voters to show identification unless they are voting for the first time.

Vote—or Else?

Another debate within voting rights is whether or not voting should become mandatory, rather than voluntary. Should people have to vote or otherwise be punished in some way? Some people say yes—others say no. Some other countries, such as Singapore, Austria, and Belgium, have mandatory voting. Australia fines anyone who doesn't vote unless they have a solid reason for it. The first

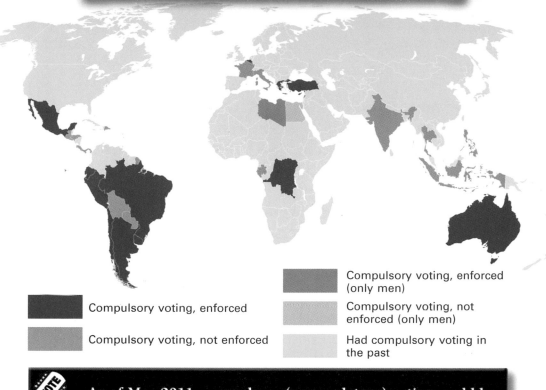

Compulsory voting, enforced

Compulsory voting, not enforced

Compulsory voting, enforced (only men)

Compulsory voting, not enforced (only men)

Had compulsory voting in the past

As of May 2011, compulsory (or mandatory) voting could be found across the globe. The United States does not have mandatory voting.

time it happens, the fee is only about $15—but it goes up for each election missed.

The voter turnout in the United States is surprisingly low—the most active states rarely average more than 50 percent, and many more are between 30 and 40 percent. Would punishing non-voters help raise that percentage closer to Australia's 95 percent rate? No one is sure. One poll done through ABC News showed that 72 percent of Americans were against any law that would require them to vote.[4] Many feel that compulsory voting is taking away a freedom and turning it into a chore. There is also debate about whether forcing people to vote will result in honest and sincere votes or something blindly done just to get it over with. Others believe that making it mandatory would be just like paying taxes—

something you have to do as part of your responsibility as a U.S. citizen. For now, the idea will continue to be debated in political circles.

Another Amendment?

Over the years, a number of amendments have been added to the Constitution regarding voting. The Fifteenth Amendment gave the right to vote to male citizens of all races. The Nineteenth Amendment gave the voting right to women. The Twenty-fourth Amendment brought an end to using poll taxes at elections. The Twenty-sixth Amendment, passed in 1971, allowed all citizens over the age of 18 the right to vote in local, state, and federal elections. Until the amendment, some states required voters to be 21 years old.

There is another amendment that some people are determined should be added to the Constitution. It is known as the Right to Vote amendment. The right to vote, as mentioned earlier, is not federally protected and guaranteed as a part of the U.S. Constitution. Less than a dozen democracies throughout the world do not have this right written into their constitutions. Groups like Fair-Vote believe that an amendment needs to be added to cover this issue. The proposed amendment, known officially as House Joint Resolution 28, reads:

> SECTION 1. All citizens of the United States, who are eighteen years of age or older, shall have the right to vote in any public election held in the jurisdiction in which the citizen resides. The right to vote shall not be denied or abridged by the United States, any State, or any other public or private person or entity, except that the United States or any State may establish regulations narrowly tailored to produce efficient and honest elections.
>
> SECTION 2. Each State shall administer public elections in the State in accordance with election performance standards established by the Congress. The Congress shall reconsider such election performance standards at least once every four years to determine if higher standards should be established to reflect improvements in methods and practices regarding the administration of elections.

SECTION 3. Each State shall provide any eligible voter the opportunity to register and vote on the day of any public election.

SECTION 4. The Congress shall have power to enforce this article by appropriate legislation.[5]

For more than 200 years, people have been fighting for their rights within the United States of America. First it was simply the right to have their own country with their own government—one in which they would have a voice. Then, once some of its citizens were able to speak out, the battle to allow all of its citizens to do so began. It was a long and difficult road, traveled with passion and determination. Thanks to the dedication of many people, today, all genders and races can vote once they reach the age of 18. But it is clear that this does not mean the battles are over.

Questions still surround the right to vote. Does it belong to everyone or should there be limits on who the people are, where they were born, or where they live now? Is casting a vote something Americans have the right to do today but might be required to do tomorrow? Since this right is not currently federally protected within the Constitution, should it be?

Chances are that people will continue to debate all of these issues. Voting is such an important right that any decision involving it deserves a great deal of thought, argument, and time. In the meantime, voting will remain a right that is given to American citizens when they turn 18. Knowing the long, hard work that went into making sure you can cast your vote is your key to making a wise decision—and using your voice.

How many people do you think vote each year in presidential elections? It might be fewer than you think. For example in 2010, the states with the highest voter turnout were Maine and Minnesota. In these states, 55.5 percent of the eligible population voted. That is just over half. The state with the lowest voter turnout was Texas, at 32.3 percent. That is just under one third.[6]

1620   Pilgrims aboard *The Mayflower* sail to North America to escape religious persecution in England.

1773   American colonists dump British tea into Boston Harbor, crying, "No taxation without representation."

1787   The U.S. Constitution is written. Voting rights are granted to adult white males who are landowners.

1848   Seneca Falls Convention in New York is the first national convention for women's suffrage.

1851   Sojourner Truth asks, "Ain't I a woman?" at the Women's Convention.

1857   In the Dred Scott case, the U.S. Supreme Court rules that Congress does not have the right to outlaw slavery in the states. It also rules that slaves are not citizens.

1863   Abraham Lincoln's Emancipation Proclamation frees all the slaves in the U.S.

1866   The Civil Rights Act grants citizenship to all native-born Americans, but this does not yet include the right to vote. It also does not include Native Americans.

1868   The Fourteenth Amendment grants citizenship to everyone born in the United States and protects citizens' civil and political rights.

1870   The Fifteenth Amendment, giving African American men the equal right to vote, is ratified; the next day, Thomas Mundy Peterson becomes the first African American to vote.

1872   Susan B. Anthony and several other women vote for U.S. president. The next year, Anthony is found guilty of illegal voting.

1920   The Nineteenth Amendment is passed, granting women the right to vote.

1924   Native Americans are granted citizenship, and with that, they have the right to vote.

1937   The U.S. Supreme Court rules to uphold the constitutionality of poll taxes in Georgia.

1954   The U.S. Supreme Court rules in *Brown v. Board of Education* that racial segregation in schools is unconstitutional.

1957   Congress passes the Civil Rights Act of 1957, which allows the U.S. Attorney General the power to bring lawsuits on behalf of African Americans who have been denied the right to vote.

1960   Congress passes the Civil Rights Act of 1960, which allows African Americans whose earlier voter registrations were rejected to apply to federal court.

1964   Three civil rights workers (James E. Chaney, Andrew Goodman, and Michael Schwerner) are murdered by the Ku Klux Klan. The men had been working to register black voters in Mississippi. Poll taxes are outlawed.

1965   The three marches across the Pettus Bridge in Selma, Alabama, are held in March. The first one ends in violence. The second one, led by Martin Luther King Jr., does not get past the bridge. The third one reaches Montgomery and is 25,000 people strong. The march is a large part of why President Lyndon B. Johnson signs a new voting rights act a few months later. This law makes it easier for Southern blacks to register to vote.

1966 The Supreme Court declares all poll taxes are unconstitutional because they violate the equal protection clause of the Fourteenth Amendment.

1971 The Twenty-sixth Amendment gives 18-year-olds the right to vote.

1974 The U.S. Supreme Court rules that states may deny convicted felons the right to vote.

1990 The Americans with Disabilities Act is passed by Congress; it requires election workers and polling sites to make it possible for people with disabilities to vote.

1993 President Bill Clinton signs the National Voter Registration Act, which makes it easy to register to vote at state agencies.

2002 Congress passes the Help America Vote Act to replaced outdated voting systems, which had caused votes to be disqualified.

2005 U.S. Representative Jesse Jackson Jr. proposes House Joint Resolution 28, which calls for a guarantee of voting rights in the Constitution.

2009 Congress establishes the Military and Overseas Voter Empowerment Act for overseas voters; Senator Russell Feingold and Representative John Conyers propose the Democracy Restoration Act.

2012 A vote on the Democracy Restoration Act is expected.

Chapter Notes

Chapter 1. Early Voting Rights
1. U.S. Department of State, *Outline of U.S. Government,* "Chapter 8, Government of the People: The Role of the Citizen," http://infousa.state.gov/media/overview/ch8.html
2. "Naturalization Act of 1790," Arizona Constitutional Republic Party, http://www.constitutionalrepublicparty.org/constitution-of-the-united-states-of-america/article-i/naturalization-act-of-1790/

Chapter 2. Blacks and Citizenship Rights
1. PBS: "Dred Scott's Fight for Freedom, 1846–1857," http://www.pbs.org/wgbh/aia/part4/4p2932.html
2. "The Emancipation Proclamation, January 1, 1963, By the President of the United States of America"; http://www.nps.gov/ncro/anti/emancipation.html
3. The U.S. Constitution, Amendment 15, http://www.usconstitution.net/const.html

Chapter 3. Blacks and the Right to Vote
1. Edward Rothstein, "Four Men, a Counter and Soon, Revolution," *The New York Times,* January 31, 2010, http://www.nytimes.com/2010/02/01/arts/design/01museum.html?pagewanted=all
2. National Museum of American History, "Goldsboro Lunch Counter," http://americanhistory.si.edu/news/factsheet.cfm?key=30&newskey=53

3. Rothstein.
4. *We Shall Overcome*: "Selma-to-Montgomery March," National Park Service, http://www.nps.gov/nr/travel/civilrights/al4.htm
5. "President Lyndon B. Johnson's Remarks in the Capitol Rotunda at the Signing of the Voting Rights Act, August 6, 1965," Lyndon Baines Johnson Library and Museum, http://www.lbjlib.utexas.edu/johnson/archives.hom/speeches.hom/650806.asp

Chapter 4. Women and the Right to Vote

1. *Internet Modern History Sourcebook*: Modern History Sourcebook: Sojourner Truth: "Ain't I a Woman?" December 1851, Women's Convention, Akron, Ohio, http://www.fordham.edu/halsall/mod/sojtruth-woman.asp
2. *Internet Modern History Sourcebook*: The Declaration of Sentiments, Seneca Falls Conference, 1848, http://www.fordham.edu/halsall/mod/senecafalls.asp
3. Doug Linder, *Famous American Trials,* "The Trial of Susan B. Anthony for Illegal Voting," University of Missouri-Kansas City School of Law, 2001, http://law2.umkc.edu/faculty/projects/ftrials/anthony/sbaaccount.html
4. Karen D. Smith, "Overcoming Opposition," *Amarillo Globe-News,* March 31, 1999, http://amarillo.com/stories/033199/fri_fandn033199-23.shtml
5. Native American Citizenship, "1924 Indian Citizenship Act," Nebraska Studies.org, http://www.nebraskastudies.org/0700/frameset_reset.html?http://www.nebraskastudies.org/0700/stories/0701_0146.html

Chapter 5. Current Voting Issues

1. Deborah Sontag, "Noncitizens and Right to Vote; Advocates for Immigrants Explore Opening Up Balloting," *The New York Times,* July 31, 1992, http://www.nytimes.com/1992/07/31/nyregion/noncitizens-right-vote-advocates-for-immigrants-explore-opening-up-balloting.html?pagewanted=all&src=pm
2. Michael Cooper, "New State Rules Raising Hurdles at Voting Booth," *The New York Times,* October 2, 2011, http://www.nytimes.com/2011/10/03/us/new-state-laws-are-limiting-access-for-voters.html
3. Ibid.
4. Dalia Sussman, "Poll: Americans Oppose a Law That Would Make Voting Compulsory," *ABC News,* June 11, 2004, http://abcnews.go.com/sections/politics/Polls/No_vote_poll_040611.html
5. Joint Resolution: FairVote Archives, "Text of House Joint Resolution Res. 28, The Right to Vote Amendment," updated December 2009, http://archive.fairvote.org/?page=214
6. United States Elections Project: "2010 General Election Turnout Rates," January 21, 2011, http://elections.gmu.edu/Turnout_2010G.html

Books

Engdahl, Sylvia. *Amendment XXVI: Lowering the Voting Age.* Farmington Hills, MI: Greenhaven Press, 2009.

Gann, Marjorie. *Five Thousand Years of Slavery.* Toronto, Ontario: Tundra Books, 2011.

Lansford, Tom. *Voting Rights.* Farmington Hills, MI: Greenhaven Press, 2008.

Norgren, Jill. *Belva Lockwood: Equal Rights Pioneer.* Minneapolis, MN: Twenty-First Century Books, 2008.

Orr, Tamra. *Susan B. Anthony.* Hockessin, DE: Mitchell Lane Publishers, 2006.

Osborne, Linda Barrett. *Miles to Go for Freedom: Segregation and Civil Rights in the Jim Crow Years.* New York: Abrams Books for Young Readers, 2012.

Works Consulted

Cooper, Michael. "New State Rules Raising Hurdles at Voting Booth." *The New York Times,* October 2, 2011.

FairVote: "The Right to Vote Amendment." http://www.fairvote.org/right-to-vote-amendment

Griffith, Benjamin. *America Votes! A Guide to Modern Election Law and Voting Rights.* Washington, D.C.: American Bar Association, 2008.

Halsall, Paul. "Modern History Sourcebook: Sojourner Truth: 'Ain't I a Woman?' December 1851." Fordham University. http://www.fordham.edu/halsall/mod/sojtruth-woman.asp

Help America Vote Act. http://www.votingaccess.org/

The Library of Congress: African American Odyssey. http://memory.loc.gov/ammem/aaohtml/exhibit/aointro.html

The Library of Congress: Votes for Women: Selections from the Woman Suffrage Association Collection, 1848–1921. http://memory.loc.gov/ammem/naw/nawshome.html

Reclaim Democracy: "A Proposed Amendment to Establish a Constitutional Right to Vote in America." http://reclaimdemocracy.org/political_reform/amendment_constitutional_voting_right.html

Sheridan, Michael. "King Abullah: Saudi Women Can Vote, Hold Elected Office in 2015." *The New York Daily News,* September 25, 2011.

Smith, Karen D. "Overcoming Opposition." *Amarillo Globe-News,* March 31, 1999. http://amarillo.com/stories/033199/fri_fandn033199-23.shtml

Sontag, Deborah. "Noncitizens and Right to Vote; Advocates for Immigrants Explore Opening Up Balloting." *The New York Times,* July 31, 1992.

Thernstrom, Abigail. *Voting Rights—and Wrongs: The Elusive Quest for Racially Fair Elections.* Washington, DC: AEI Press, 2009.

United States Elections Project. "2010 General Election Turnout Rates." January 28, 2011. http://elections.gmu.edu/Turnout_2010G.html

U.S. Department of State. Outline of U.S. Government. http://infousa.state.gov/media/overview/media_homepage.html#ch1

On the Internet

Ben's Guide to the U.S. Government: The Election Process
    http://bensguide.gpo.gov/9-12/election/
PBS: The Democracy Project
    http://pbskids.org/democracy/govandme/
Peck, Ira. "Susan B. Anthony Dares to Vote!" *Junior Scholastic,* March 10,
    1989. http://www.scholastic.com/browse/article.jsp?id=4973
ZOOM Out the Vote!
    http://pbskids.org/zoom/fromyou/elections/elections101.html

Glossary

abolitionist (ab-uh-LIH-shuh-nist)—A person who fought for the end
    of slavery during the Civil War era.
criminal disenfranchisement (KRIH-mih-nul dis-en-FRAN-chyz-
    munt)—The process of denying voting rights to convicted felons.
democracy (deh-MAH-kruh-see)—A form of government in which
    people vote for their leaders.
felon (FEH-lun)—A person who has committed a serious crime, or
    felony (FEH-luh-nee).
gender (JEN-dur)—A person's sex (male or female).
hunger strike (HUN-gur STRYK)—Going without any kind of food
    on purpose, often to make a political statement.
literacy test (LIH-tuh-ruh-see TEST)—A test to find out if a person
    can read and understand what they read.
mandatory (MAN-dah-tor-ee)—Required or necessary.
poll tax (POHL TAKS)—A fee paid before voting.
ratification (rah-tih-fih-KAY-shun)—The act of formally approving (a
    law).
registrar (REH-jis-trar)—A person who keeps official records or
    documents.
suffragist (SUH-fruh-jist)—A person who fought for women's right
    to vote.
voter fraud (VOH-ter FRAWD)—Lying at the polls, especially about
    one's identity.

About the
Author

Tamra Orr is a full-time writer and author. She is mother to four and an avid reader and letter writer. Orr has written more than 300 nonfiction books for young readers, including biographies of former presidents and many other historical subjects. She lives in Oregon, one of two states that relies on mailed-in votes rather than standing in line at a voting booth.